A Picnic

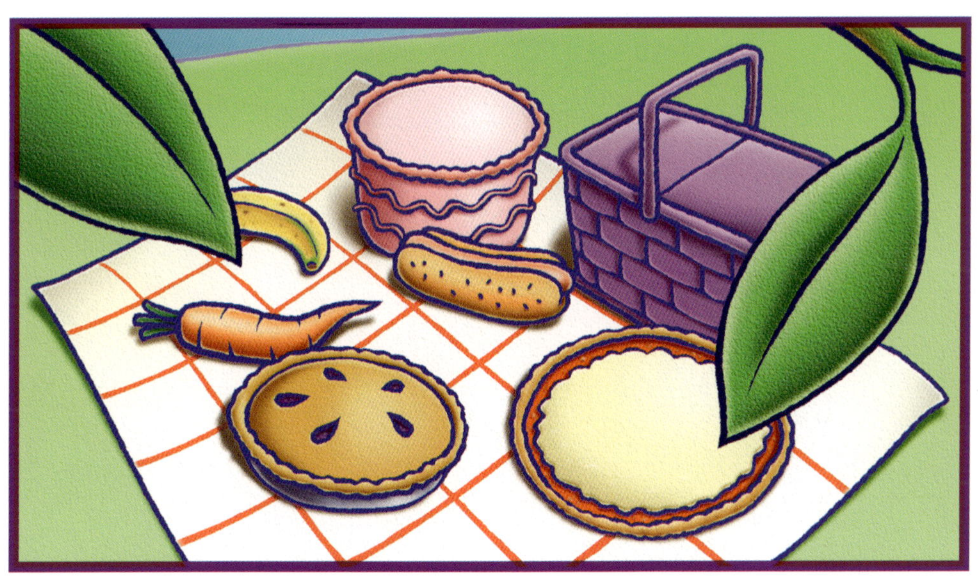

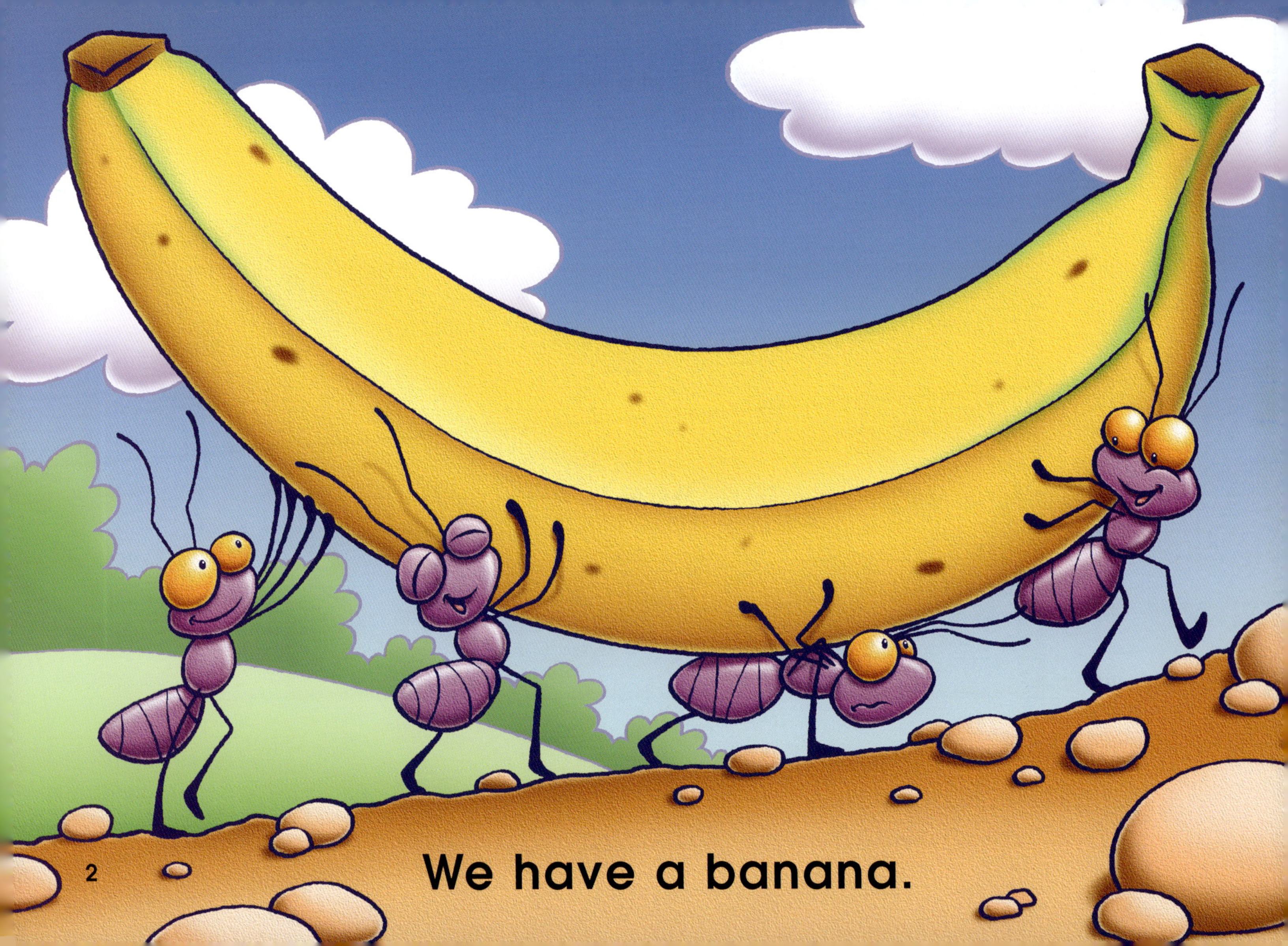

We have a banana.

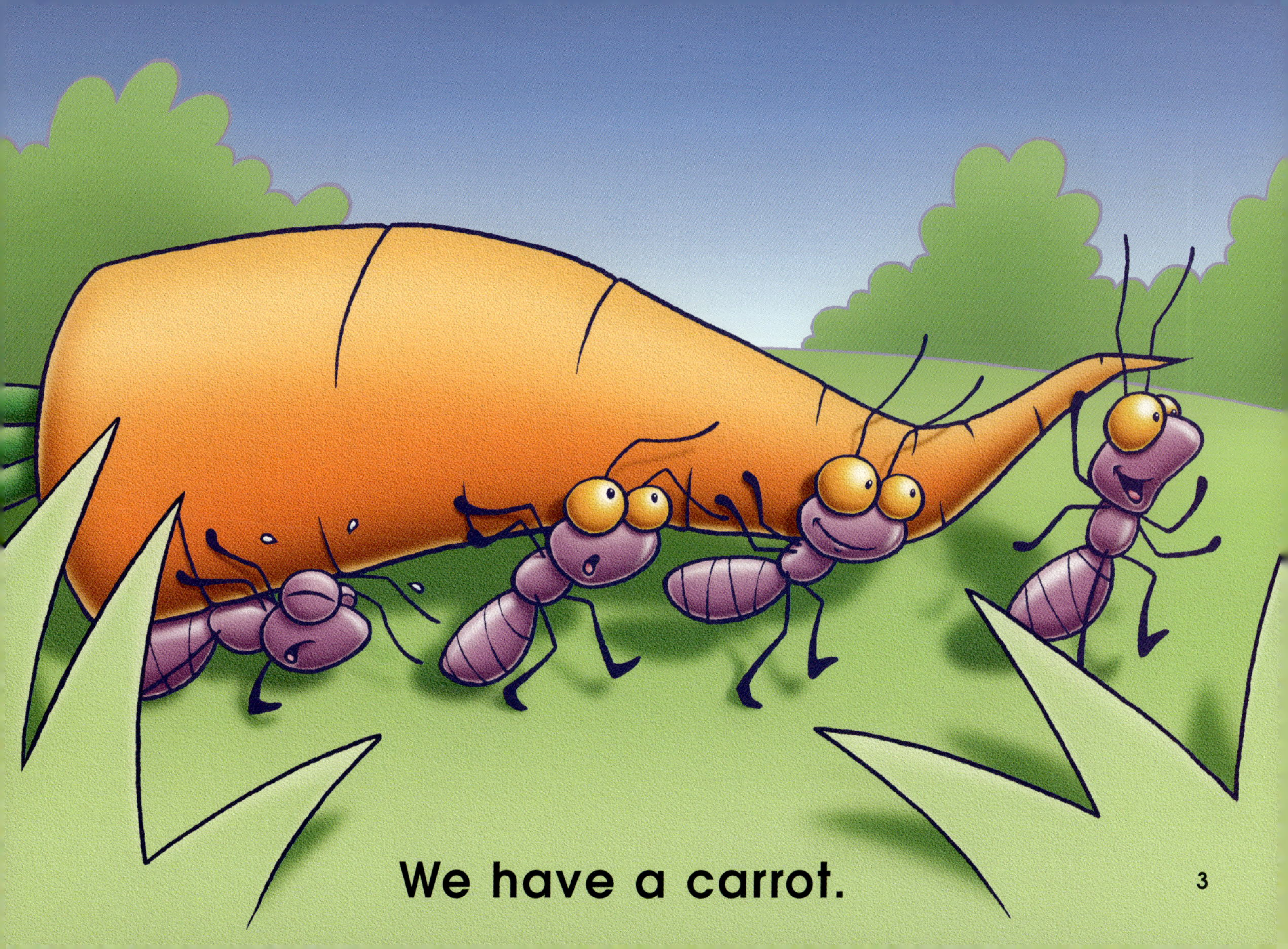

We have a carrot.

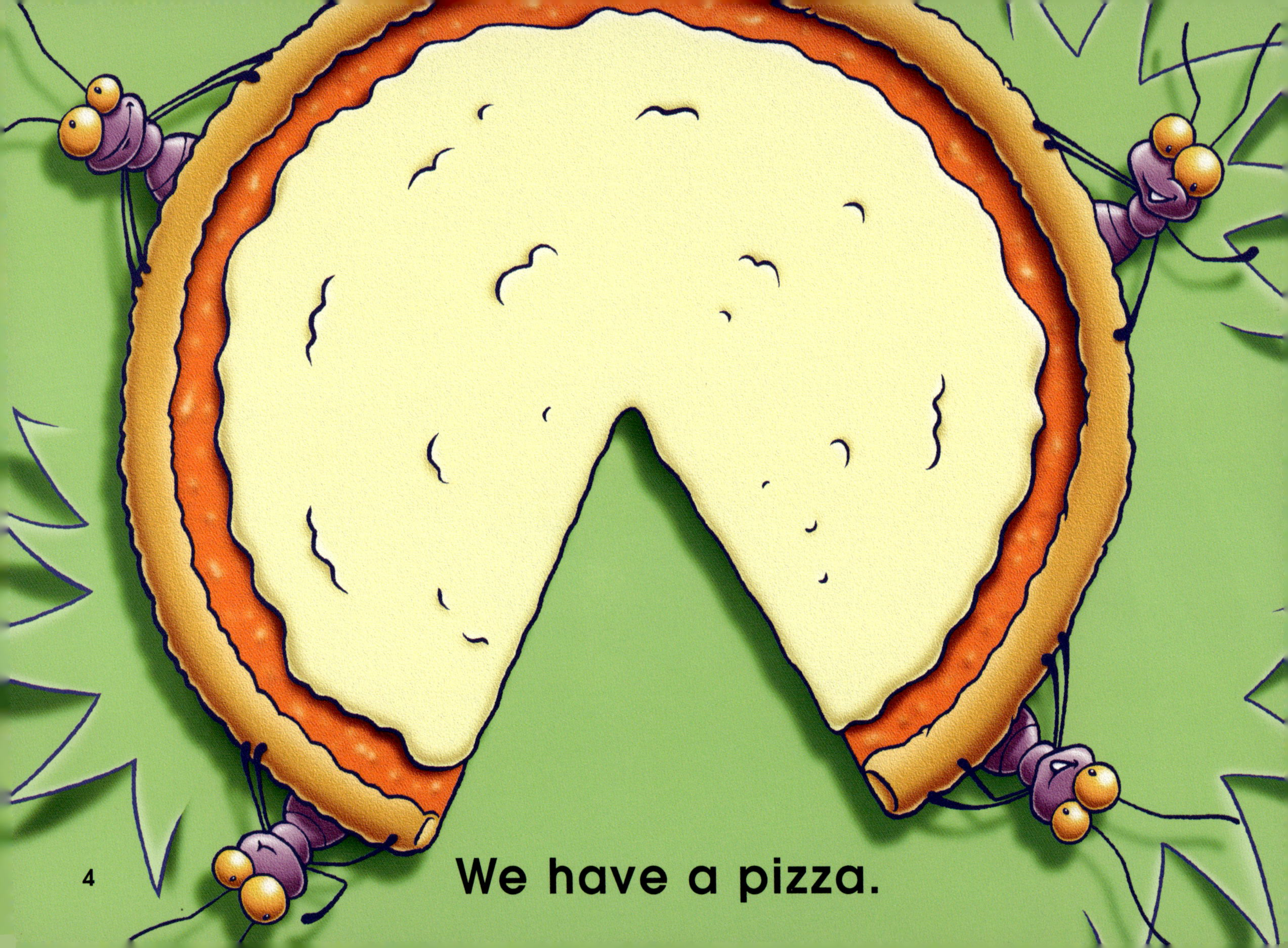

We have a pizza.

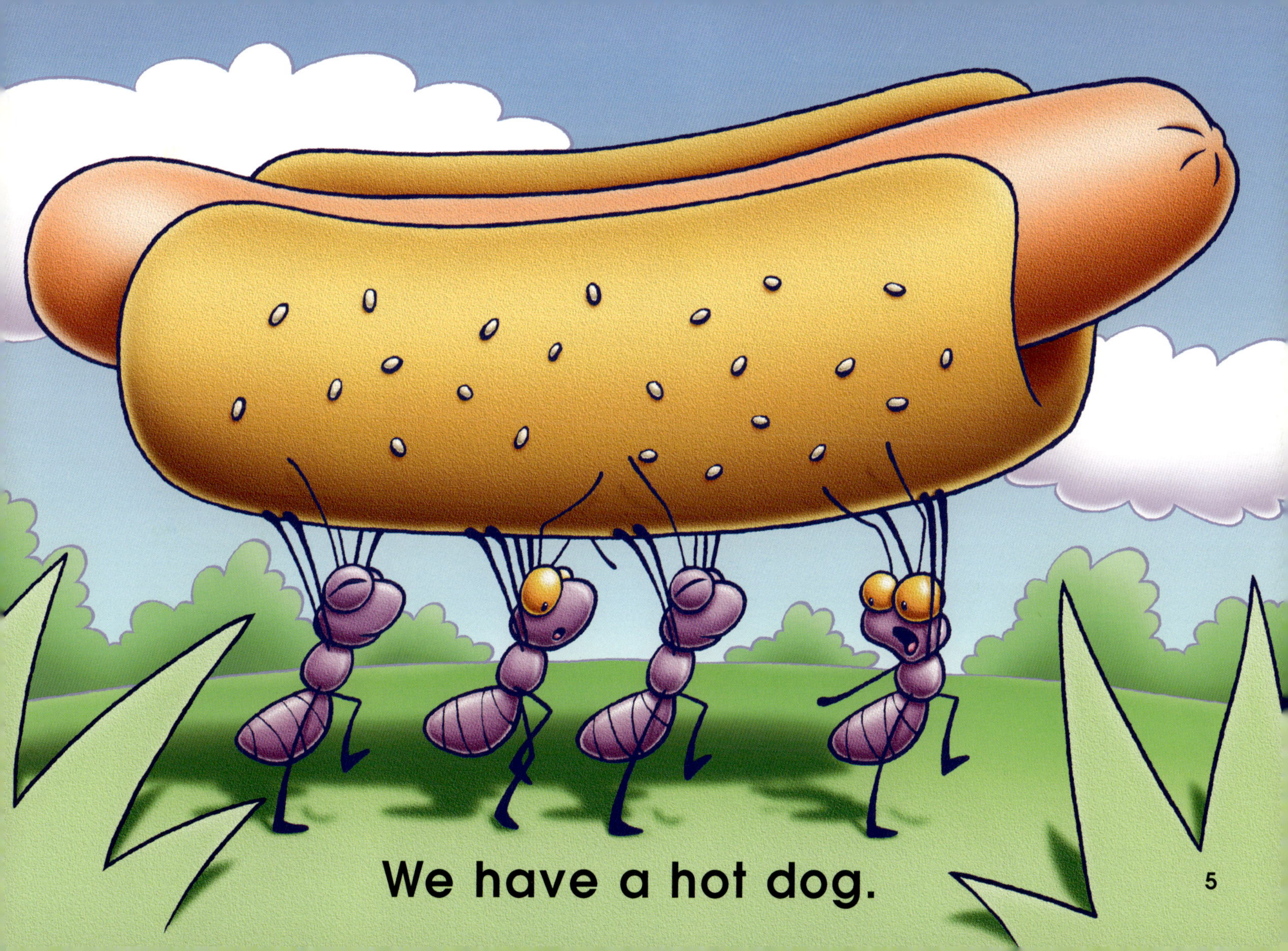

We have a hot dog.

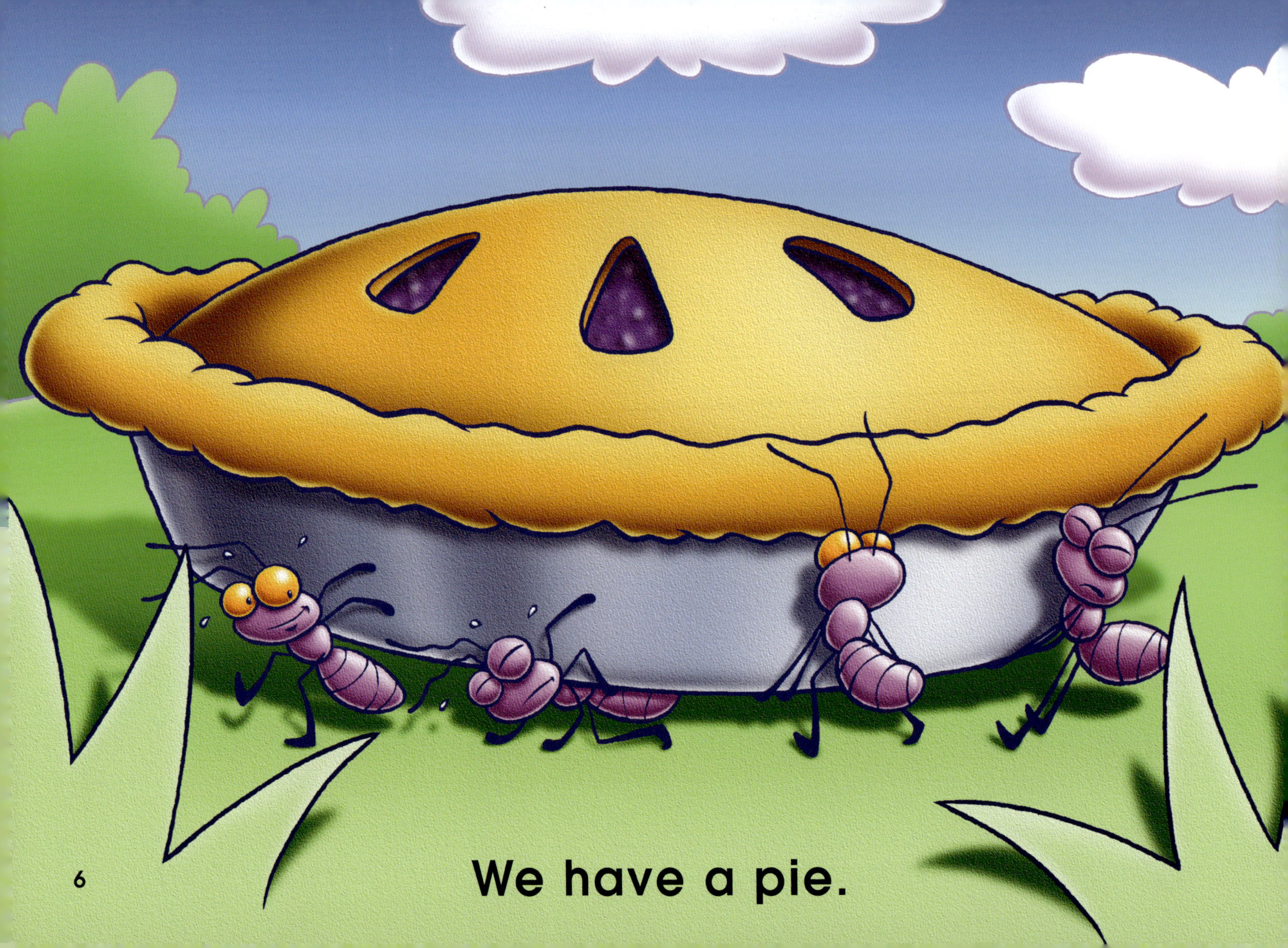

We have a pie.

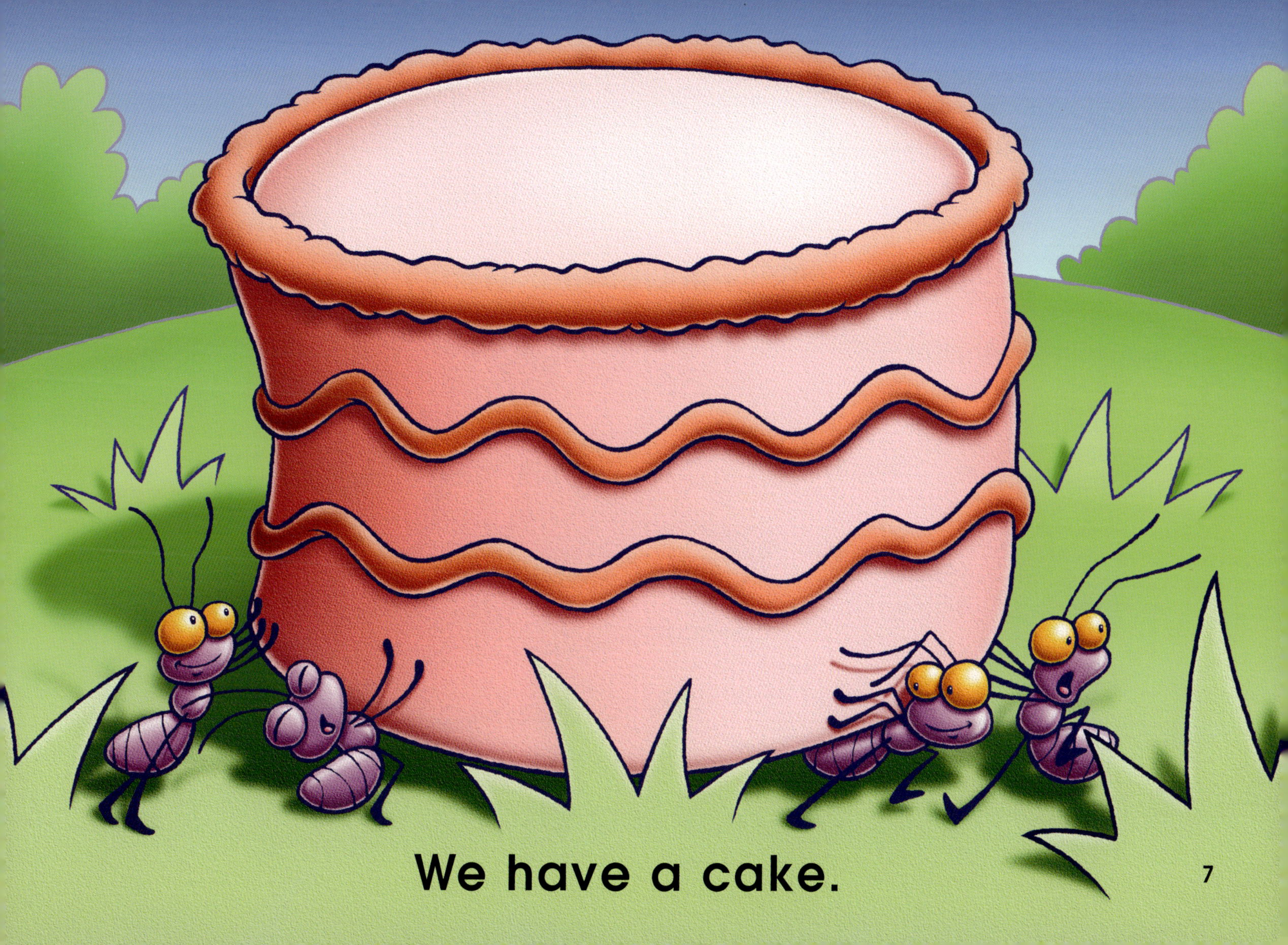

We have a cake.

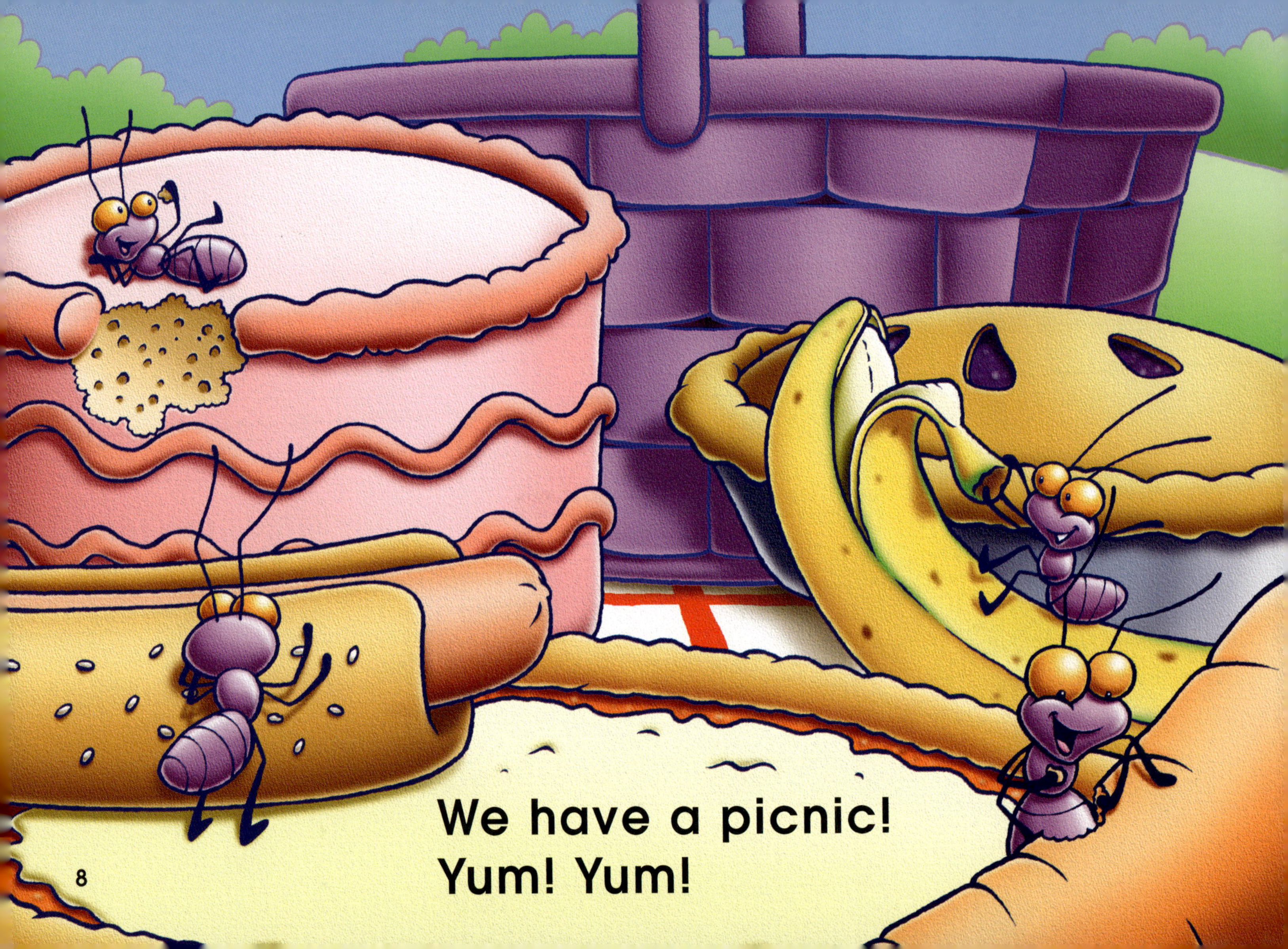

We have a picnic!
Yum! Yum!